Contents

Any words appearing in bold, **like this**, are explained in the Glossary.

Was your pet once wild?

Did you know that your pet dog is closely related to wild animals? Finding out more about your dog's wild relatives will help you give it a better life.

The largest wild dog is the wolf. A wolf can weigh up to 80 kilograms. That is the same as a full-grown person.

Wolves cannot be tamed like **domestic** dogs.

4

The Wild Side of Pet
Dogs

Jo Waters

www.raintreepublishers.co.uk
Visit our website to find out more information about **Raintree** books.

To order:
☎ Phone 44 (0) 1865 888112
🗎 Send a fax to 44 (0) 1865 314091
💻 Visit the Raintree Bookshop at **www.raintreepublishers.co.uk** to browse our catalogue and order online.

First published in Great Britain by Raintree, Halley Court, Jordan Hill, Oxford OX2 8EJ, part of Harcourt Education.
Raintree is a registered trademark of Harcourt Education Ltd.

Editorial: Melanie Copland and Saskia Besier
Design: Richard Parker and
Tinstar Design Ltd (www.tinstar.co.uk)
Picture Research: Maria Joannou and Alison Prior
Production: Duncan Gilbert

Originated by Ambassador Litho Ltd
Printed and bound in China by South China Printing Company

The paper used to print this book comes from sustainable resources.

ISBN 1 844 43480 X (hardback)
08 07 06 05 04
10 9 8 7 6 5 4 3 2 1

ISBN 1 844 43487 7 (paperback)
09 08 07 06 05
10 9 8 7 6 5 4 3 2 1

British Library Cataloguing in Publication Data
Waters, Jo
The Wild Side of Pet Dogs
636.7
A full catalogue record for this book is available from the British Library.

Acknowledgements
The publishers would like to thank the following for permission to reproduce photographs: Animal Photography pp. 7, 11, 27 (Sally Anne Thompson); Ardea p. 5 top; Bruce Coleman Collection pp. 6 (Joe McDonald), 23 (J & P Wegner), 24 (W S Paton); Getty Images p. 29 (Photodisc); Heather Angel p. 12 (C A Henley); Nature Picture Library p. 22 (S King); NHPA pp. 4 (A Rouse), 10 (T Kitchin & V Hurst), 16 (Martin Harvey), 18 (M Danegger), 19 (R Wu), 28 (R Kirchner); Oxford Scientific Films p. 5 bot (T Jackson); Photodisc p. 15; Photographers Direct p. 14; RSPCA Photolibrary p. 9; Science Photo Library p. 26 (Clem Haagner); Tudor Photography/Harcourt Education Ltd pp. 13, 17, 21, 25.

Cover photograph of a border collie, reproduced with permission of NHPA (Lady Philippa Scott). Inset cover photograph of a timber wolf reproduced with permission of NHPA (David Middleton).

The publishers would like to thank Michaela Miller for her assistance in the preparation of this book.

Every effort has been made to contact copyright holders of any material reproduced in this book. Any omissions will be rectified in subsequent printings if notice is given to the publishers.

Pet dogs can be great companions and join in with family life. Not all dogs are friendly pets though and some can be **aggressive**. Also, not all dogs are happy around children. Always check with a dog's owner before you touch it.

Looking after

Dogs need a lot of care and attention but this can be fun. Dogs must be walked regularly. In the wild, dogs are moving and hunting most of the time. Wolves can travel 50 kilometres (30 miles) each day. Your pet dog still has **instincts**, but cannot go off roaming. You need to help it keep fit and healthy.

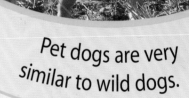

Pet dogs are very similar to wild dogs.

Types of dog

Wolves are wild dogs. There are grey wolves, Abyssinian wolves and red wolves.

Feral dogs

As well as true wild dogs, there are also pet dogs that have returned to live in the wild. We call these dogs 'feral'.

Coyotes are slim dogs with bushy tails and pointed **muzzles**. Common jackals are smaller and lighter with large, pointed ears.

Foxes are small wild dogs. Many, like the ones in the UK and USA, have a deep red coat and a bushy tail.

Dingoes are Australian wild dogs. They have sandy coloured, short coats.

This Arctic fox's fur changes colour from summer to winter.

Different dogs suit different people. Do you have the time to groom a dog every day?

Mongrels and pedigrees

There are lots of types of **domestic** dog. There are purebred dogs, called pedigree dogs. There are mixed breed dogs, called mongrels. Dogs can be huge like St Bernards or tiny like chihuahuas.

Allergies

Some people cannot keep dogs because they are **allergic** to their hairs. You should make sure that you do not have an allergy before deciding to get a dog.

Where are dogs from?

Wild dogs live all over the world. Grey wolves are found in North America, Russia, Northern Europe and Asia. Other types of wolf are found in Mexico and Africa.

Foxes live in many places and are common in the UK and North America. Coyotes live in the USA and Canada. Jackals live in Africa, Europe, India and the Middle East. Dingoes live in Australia and Asia.

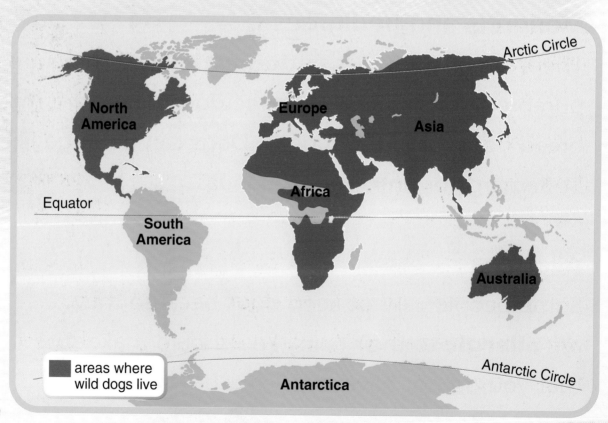

Arctic Circle

North America

Europe

Asia

Africa

Equator

South America

Australia

areas where wild dogs live

Antarctic Circle

Antarctica

This map shows where wild dogs can be found.

When you get a dog, try to buy it from a good **breeder**. Always go to see the puppies with their mother before you buy one. If the mother is healthy, happy and friendly, your puppy probably will be too.

This rescue centre dog needs a new home.

Rescue dogs

It can be very rewarding to adopt a dog from an animal rescue centre. Sometimes dogs lose their home through no fault of their own. Many dogs are abandoned when they grow bigger or become too much work.

Living in groups

Wild dogs usually live in packs. African wild dogs live in family packs like wolves. Golden jackals live in pairs rather than packs.

Communication

Most wild dogs greet each other with sniffs and licks. They howl, bark or yelp to warn of danger and to **communicate**. Jackals are very noisy and communicate in yaps and yelps.

Grey wolves live in packs of ten or more.

These dogs are checking each other out.

Most pet dogs will be happy living with other dogs. However, if a dog has been alone since it was young, it may not like being around other dogs. If you get a rescue dog, always find out how it behaves with other animals.

Barking

Pet dogs communicate with you in the same way that wild dogs communicate with their pack. A bark is usually a warning to tell you something is near. Noises like grumbles and whining are to get attention.

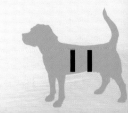

Dog habitats

Different types of wild dog have **adapted** to live in different **environments**. Grey wolves like to live in forests and they are well adapted to cold. They even live in the Arctic. In contrast, the Abyssinian wolf lives in the hot deserts of Ethiopia.

Territory

Dogs in a pack usually all live together in their own **territory**. Inside their territory, the dogs roam around and hunt. They also choose somewhere special to rest and sleep. Many have dens underground or in sheltered spots of a forest.

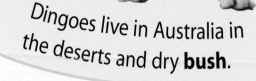

Dingoes live in Australia in the deserts and dry **bush**.

House training

Wild dogs never go to
the toilet in their dens.
Your pet dog will learn that it
should wee outside its den – your house!

Your dog may wee on the fence, or pots!
It does this to mark its territory.

Your dog will treat your garden as its territory.
The garden needs to be safely fenced so the
dog cannot get out.

13

Dog anatomy

All dogs have the same basic **anatomy** or body parts. Wild dogs have very strong jaws. They also have sharp **canine** teeth for killing **prey** and tearing meat.

Wild dogs are active a lot of the time. African wild dogs are very lean and strong. They have broad heads and short **muzzles**. They can run at about 50 kilometres (30 miles) per hour and keep on going for hours.

Claws are useful for hunting, gripping the ground when running, and digging.

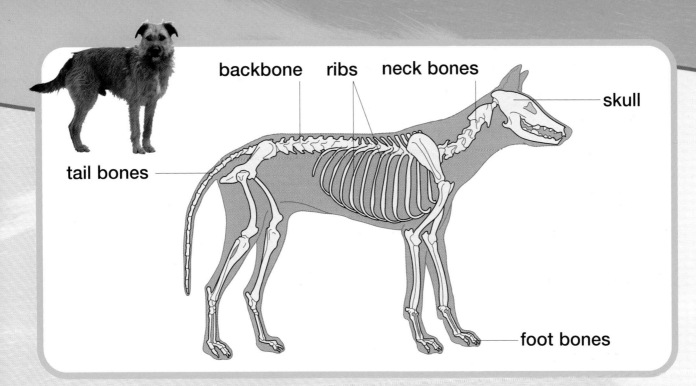

This drawing shows the basic skeleton of a dog.

Most **domestic** dogs have hairy coats, teeth, claws, a tail and sharp senses. There are a few hairless dogs like the toy Mexican hairless.

Muscles

Some pet dogs have more muscles than others. Some run very quickly for short bursts, like the greyhound. Other dogs, like border collies, can keep running for hours at a time.

Pet dogs have claws and pads just like wild dogs. Many dogs will dig in the garden if they can. This is **instinctive** wild behaviour, like digging for dens.

Senses

Wild dogs use their senses all the time. They can hear four times better than humans. They can hear very high sounds made by small animals.

Wild dogs' eyes are wide apart at the front of their head. They can see tiny movements a long way away.

Pack smell

Dogs use smell to recognize their **territory**. Dogs in the same pack recognize each other by smell. Wild dogs also use their excellent sense of smell to find **prey**.

African wild dogs have big furry ears that catch sounds. The ears can move to listen in different directions.

When you blow a dog whistle, you cannot hear it but the dog can.

Dogs see differently from humans. They rely more on shapes and movement. They also have difficulty telling colours apart. They recognize you by shape and smell more than the colour of your hair or clothes.

Sniffing

Domestic dogs have kept their amazing sense of smell. They use it to recognize food, people, other dogs and even places. Your dog will probably sniff you when you come home to smell where you have been.

Movement

Dogs use their muscles to move their legs. The back legs do most of the work when the dog is walking or running. The front legs are used as brakes and to keep them steady. The muscles in dogs' backs allow them to jump and help them to run.

Different muscles

There are different types of muscle called fast and slow twitch muscles. These allow dogs to do different things. Wolves will use their slow twitch muscles to keep moving steadily for hours.

A fox will use its fast twitch muscles for short sprints and quick leaps.

Exercise

Pet dogs must have enough space to move around and exercise in. Think very carefully before getting a pet dog. You may need a large garden and all dogs need regular exercise.

Pet dogs and wild dogs use their muscles to run and leap.

It is important that your dog learns to walk on a lead. A dog should be on a lead near people, in any public place and anywhere with other animals.

Paddling

Most dogs can swim. Some, like labradors, love swimming! They paddle with all four feet whilst keeping their noses clear of the water to breathe.

What do dogs eat?

Wild dogs hunt and catch **prey** for food. Grey wolves will kill small animals like hares and rabbits, but they also kill deer and other large animals.

Omnivores

Most dogs will eat any food that is available, including small amounts of plants or vegetables. This makes them **omnivores**.

Some dogs, like African wild dogs only eat meat. Jackals eat reptiles, birds, fruit and even insects. They will also **scavenge**. Coyotes and foxes will come into towns and eat out of bins or attack pets.

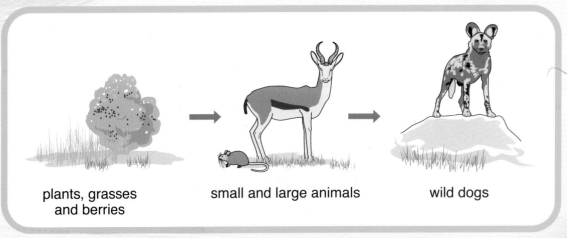

plants, grasses and berries   small and large animals   wild dogs

This is how wild dogs fit into a **food chain**.

Make sure you know what to feed your dog. Soft dog foods in cans or foil packets usually contain fresh meat or fish. There are also dried foods.

Dogs should always have some hard food, like biscuits or chews, to keep their teeth clean and healthy. They also need lots of clean water to drink.

Bad foods

*Never give dogs chocolate. It can make them very sick. Bones can splinter and get stuck in a dog's mouth or insides. Some dogs are **allergic** to beef and pork.*

Dogs need a mixture of soft and hard foods.

Wild dogs use different techniques to catch their **prey**. Wolves run their prey down. They separate an animal from its herd and chase it until it is exhausted.

Coyotes track their prey using their sharp sense of smell. They stalk the animal and then pounce. Jackals can hunt alone or in groups. When they hunt, they howl to each other to keep in touch.

Dingoes hunt at night. When they catch something, they may bury it and come back to it later.

Agility training keeps your dog fit and makes it use its brain as well.

Chasing instincts

Pet dogs still have wild hunting **instincts**. Some dogs will try to chase rabbits and cats. If you are around other animals, always keep your dog on a lead.

Playtime

Play helps wild dogs to learn hunting skills. Pet dogs also love to play. When your dog chases and catches a ball, it sees the toy as its prey. Playing also helps you bond with your dog as it will think of you as part of the hunting pack.

Sleeping

All dogs need to sleep, and most sleep a lot. It is important for dogs to get lots of sleep when they are young as it helps them grow.

Dingoes hunt mostly at night. They can also be active during the day, but they still need plenty of sleep in the daytime.

Dens

Many wild dogs, like wolves, sleep and rest in dens. They dig these out of the ground or under tree roots, or find a hidden space like a cave. Foxes also have dens where they sleep, rest and give birth to their young.

Many foxes, like this one, live in cities.

Your pet needs a bed to rest. A dog's bed is like its den in the wild, so it needs to be a safe place.

Pet dogs need to sleep quite a lot. This is natural behaviour and is what they would do in the wild. They usually have regular times when they sleep, often after meals or a walk.

Pack routine

Pet dogs usually fit in very well with your routine. They think you are their pack, so they want to do what you are doing. If you are sleeping, they will think that is what they should be doing too.

Life cycle of dogs

Male dogs are called dogs, females are called bitches. Young wild dogs are called pups. Jackals have up to six pups in a **litter**, dingoes can have eight pups and wolves and coyotes can have eleven.

Mates for life
*Wolves, jackals and many coyotes **mate** for life. This means that they stay and raise pups with the same partner for the rest of their life.*

These young black-backed jackals will help their parents look after the next litter of pups.

Puppies need their mother to do everything for them.

Both male and female pet dogs can be **neutered** to stop them from having puppies. Neutering can also stop **aggressive** behaviour from males.

Puppies

Bitches can have up to twenty pups, but they normally have from six to ten. Puppies are born helpless, deaf and blind. Their eyes open at 10 to 14 days. Pups can usually leave the litter at 8 to 10 weeks. If you get a puppy, you will need to teach it and play with it just as its mother would do.

Common problems

Wild dogs are in danger from damage to their **habitats**.

Being hunted

There used to be wolves living wild all over northern Europe, the UK and North America. Humans thought they were a threat and killed them. Wolves are now being released back into the wild in Scotland and in North Carolina, Wyoming and Idaho in the USA.

There are very few red wolves left in the wild.

In danger!
The following species of dogs are **endangered**:
• *Abyssinian wolf*
• *red wolf*
• *African wild dogs.*

Vets and vaccinations

Vaccinations are injections given by the vet to protect your pet against diseases. It is very important that your dog has all its vaccinations kept up to date.

Pet dogs can also get **mites**, fleas and worms. Ask your vet how to treat them. You should take your dog to the vet for a general health check every year.

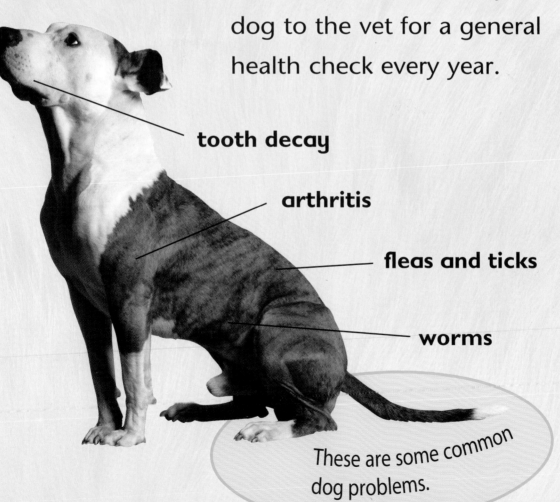

tooth decay

arthritis

fleas and ticks

worms

These are some common dog problems.

Find out for yourself

A good owner will always want to learn more about keeping a pet dog. To find out more information about dogs, you can look in other books and on the Internet.

Books to read

New Encyclopedia of the Dog, Bruce Fogle (Dorling Kindersley, 2000)

Pets: Dogs, Michaela Miller (Heinemann Library/RSPCA, 1997)

Using the Internet

Explore the Internet to find out about dogs. Websites can change, so if one of the links below no longer works, don't worry. Use a search engine, such as *www.yahooligans.com* or *www.internet4kids.com*. You could try searching with the keywords 'dog', 'pet' and 'wild dogs'.

Websites

The Kennel Club website has tips for dog care, and other links: *www.the-kennel-club.org.uk*

The PDSA website has information about how to look after dogs: *www.pdsa.org.uk* (click on 'you and your pet')

Disclaimer
All the Internet addresses (URLs) given in this book were valid at the time of going to press. However, due to the dynamic nature of the Internet, some addresses may have changed, or sites may have ceased to exist since publication. While the author and publishers regret any inconvenience this may cause readers, no responsibility for any such changes can be accepted by either the author or the publishers.

Glossary

adapted become used to living in certain conditions

aggressive angry and very unfriendly – the animal may attack

agility training special training where dogs are taught to jump things, run through tunnels and do as their owner tells them

allergic react badly to something

anatomy how the body is made

breeder someone who raises dogs

bush the forest, scrubland and desert in Australia

canine teeth the four pointy teeth near the front of the mouth

communicate to make yourself understood

domestic animals that are tame

endangered in danger of dying out or being killed

environment type of surroundings where something lives

food chain the links between different animals that feed on each other and on plants

habitat where an animal or plant lives

instinct natural behaviour which an animal is born with

litter pups that are born to the same mother at the same time

mate come together with another animal to have babies

mite small parasite that lives on another animal and sucks its blood

muzzle a dog's nose and mouth

neutered animal that has had an operation so it cannot have babies

omnivore animal that eats meat and plants

prey animals that are hunted and eaten by other animals

scavenge search for and eat dead animals, or even rubbish

territory area that an animal lives and hunts in. Animals guard their territory.

vaccinate an injection that protects an animal from disease

worm parasite that lives inside your dog and feeds off it

Index